100 Days in New York City!

Homa Parmar

Presentation by *BookLeaf Publishing*

Web: www.bookleafpub.com

E-mail: info@bookleafpub.com

ISBN: 9789357446075

First edition 2023

ACKNOWLEDGEMENT

Thank you!

To my parents and my sister for staying by my side at every step of the way.
To all the old and new souls I connected and shared moments with that helped me become the person I am today.

PREFACE

100 Days in New York City is my personal documentation of how I took control of my life and decided to make a move to a new city. This book takes you through the flows of excitement and ebbs of feeling alone at the same time. Maneuvering through this new life, I took instances from several events that happened along the course and tried to put down my feelings in that moment.

I hope the book resonates and makes you Feel your Feelings!

IT'S NEW YORK TIME OF THE YEAR!

Who know me, know this,
coming to New York has always been in the
books;
For as long as I can remember
and no matter how far stretched it looks.

Fall 2019, first few hours landing in the states
I found myself on the city streets,
Engulfed among the mad crowd
overwhelmed like a kid fantasizing treats.

Years few by with the lingering thought
of one day be able to live the dream.
I wasn't prepared then but I am ready now
Oh boy! I needed to grow and only I know how!

I spend last few months in the countryside
only to realize I needed the city to lift my pride.
Broken, lost, was going through stuff
when nights seemed longer and days were
rough!
I knew I needed myself saved
for a drastic change was what I craved!

Sealed boxes, broken leases and a loaded car,
alone but not lonely, with my courage and hope;
I drove my way to the Hudson
leaving all my darkness behind.
Reached the city at the golden hour
as it welcomed me to the grind!

Coming to the city saved me
when I thought it was all over for me!
As I write today, with just 100 days spent yet,
with so much more surely left, I bet!
It's New York time of the year
and I am all for it here!

UNIT 2302!

Saturday dusk,
reached new place.
Staring up the concrete block
seemed unreal like a long overdue case.

Got greeted with a smile,
by the doorman I never had!
Loaded carts, reserved lifts,
23rd floor and God! It wasn't that bad!

Empty crib, white walls,
as I walk in, saw a new smile.
Roommate in layman words
Friends in mine!

Living alone for so long
made me almost forget;
You do need people around
and to come home to at the end!

Open kitchen, Tall windows,
Blue couch, Ocean views,
For the next 13 months,
This is where I will be my muse!

Unpacked boxes, Opened beer cases
New faces along new spaces;
Is it just a new vibe or am I getting a feeling,
Feeling that I am finally, finally home!

PATH TO 23RD!

Winds gushing towards me,
as I waited for the 8am local;
To take me to the place,
The place I show up for my bread!

Door slides open, as I step in,
I see faces, faces screaming stories!
Stories of success, and that of the hustle,
Stories that have been lost, and some to be
found!

Some with books, some wired to their beats,
Some dressed up, some not so much!
For the tracks see no difference,
its one for all and there's nowhere to hunch!

I see the rush, I feel the drive,
all running against the time!
Be it to work, or to a loved one
or may be an explorer enjoying city at its prime!

Damped air, packed seats
poker faces with looks that would kill,
Sweaty shoulders brushing one another
bars above holding them still!

I see the hunger, I feel the drive,
People standing close, feeling unknown breathe
So close, yet so distant,
for they never will again see one another!

"Next stop is 23rd St", as I hear,
Its time to jet off and pull myself back,
For the city does not city
nor do the screeching tracks!

9 TO 5..!

Taking strides, from the path,
towards the brick where I do the math.
In the heart of the city, next to Flatiron,
where I am an architect and roar like a lion!

The Drawings, the Arts,
dodging the clients throwing darts.
Its the place I owe,
the experience it gives to fresh minds like mine!

The breaking of the ground, laying wood as I
drew,
gives a sense of pride for I worked on it too!
Demo was a success, is what I like to hear,
Construction begins, is what I like to devour.

Projects come and projects go,
but I live the process as it grows.
Could I be any more thankful
for the platform to me, it serves!

It's not just nine to five
but a place where I transform,
From a girl that was once naive
to a mindful woman that lays her own norm.

CITY ON A ROLL

There are millions souls
living under holes,
Its the shine outside
but the void beneath that it holds.

People walking like herds of wool
strolling through the narrow streets, looking Oh,
so cool!
Buildings overpower, Some tall, Some narrow
It's the concrete jungle and rightfully so.

The amalgamation of brick and steel,
makes you wonder, of the strength it bears.
Flatiron stands out with its triangular hold
dividing the ave, leading open views beyond!

Fire exits along the facade,
serve as a chill node against the graffiti wall.
Yellow taxis crowding the tar
but it's the Black coats walking that roll the ball.

Wall Street or be it union square,
you see aspirants staring, taking it all.
Its the passion in the eyes
that fuel up the soul.

The desire to be known
most definitely creeps,
For now you are in New York
The city that never sleeps!

COLD AS A WINTER DAY!

Its cold as a winter day.
But the chill I feel within
Is more than what my fur can hold!

I have this sinking feeling
Compared to the melting berg
It's hard as a rock
But seems to slide every second!

I try to hold on, hold on a little longer,
Longing for the leaves to turn golden.
But the universe seems to love,
Love the lifeless shrubs growing under.

Its cold as a winter day
Feeling chills along the spine
And here, I am just waiting for some shine!

LONG LOST WORLD!

Words matter and words weave
For that's all I have and nothing to leave,
Building myself up from the low
A community I found to serve my glow!

Friends I crossed path,
For how long? I don't even know.
But whatever it is, despite the falling
Brooklyn meets have become my calling!

Beer chugs and mindless shrugs,
Healed me more, to feel along the thugs
Its the saving of last artichoke slice
While walking along the mice!

Nothing compares to this freeness I feel,
I live each day, shedding my superficial peel,
The Highline strolls and the Holland tolls
I drive my chevy through the downtown holes.

I am happy and surely do feel alive
Like the purple pink bloom on the chive,
A cry for help is no longer needed
I feel like a freak and this time not so forbidden!

CITY GIRLS WHO WALK!

In the peak of winter
On a quest for a shining silver,
You take the train
And ride the journey uptown!

Central Park, They call it,
For me, its my new solace,
The sense of green
In the dense concrete jungle.

What more do you want
Than strolling with the girls
Random strangers, unknown stories
Reaching out for comfort curls!

All come together
To make one feel less lonely
For a moment or an hour
All worries turn holy!

Its a blessing to have a community
Rather a sense of belonging,
For it helps you thrive
In bustling cold New York hive!

NEW YORK RIZZ!

In the prime of the day
Sipping coffees at bucks!
Scanning through the thrift heaps
Trying all those last bit of fashion lucks!

Brunches bottomless,
Lunches at the grove;
Rolling through the Bryant,
As you get lost in the books nextdoor!

Laughing at the comedy underground
Or sneaking easy into the jazz,
Walking the Brooklyn across,
Smoking the magic potion, indeed getting high!

Mesmerized by the broadway rizz,
Loosing yourself in the shrooms fizz,
Baller mentality, even though you have no hops
Watching lebron at MSG surely waters the
crops!

KTown hotpots or karaoke nights
Not to forget, thrifting at the central grounds
Staring at the screens at the Times square
Nights ending with multiple shot rounds!

Its a one way ride to the city stop,
Leading to endless stuff for you to dive.
After nine to five, there is still life to live
Oh for sure, Girl! Don't be so naive!

YOU ARE THE MUSEUM!

You are the Museum,
You are the Art!
The Grandeur, The Vibe,
From MoMA to Guggenheim!

The Color, The Stroke
Makes you wonder!
It is the display or am I the shiny rock,
For Beauty lies in the eyes of that who behold!

Some look you in the eye, Pass by,
But never bother to climb the flight,
Some explore only the first floor
Cause its intimidating making your head feel
light!

Some scan all the levels
But don't understand the context,
While some only stop by
For the special exhibits, waiting already for the
Next!

But only few take time to read you through
And understand the truth within,
Those are the souls that keep coming
And will cherish your entire canvas skin!

I realized soon after,
Unlike others, I am the museum,
Its time to explore,
One display at a time!

WELCOME TO THE CITY!

Days go by, You start feeling at home,
That's when the holiday strikes making you
numb!
You feel you have your person,
Only to realize, they have their own other
reason!

Thanksgiving it was and I was in the city
Marching along the parade at Macy's!
With balloons over my head
And hand freezing inside the pocket!

A moment of lapse
And I take my arms out of the sack.
Only to reach back
To realize I lost my contact!

Phone stolen, jacket torn
Nowhere to find, among the Yorker's maze.
It was the moment, screaming at my face
Welcome to the city, in its true cold haze.

BLACK HOUR!

The Day is bright, work all done,
Pay in and a good meal to dine!

Life looks full, seems somehow fine,
But its an empty dinning, only a glass of wine!

There are faces smiling at you from miles away,
Yet one face here is masked up hiding in hay!

No longer do the greens in the bank lure,
Its the warmth of someone next to me, that
would be the cure!

LOVE BITE!

And you think,
You in the pool now,
For the sky is filed with red
Fishes swimming Here, There, Everywhere!

To be young and in love
Strolling in the streets of New York,
Arms pretzeled, fingers tangled
Kissing each others soul!

Well that was the hope
To find my own,
Alas! Found my way
Into the dating apps as I drown!

Apps are virtual, but feelings can't be,
Reality differed, landing in disappointments to
be!
Truly, apps are no better
I hope to find him sooner or later!

Just needed someone to say, I got you, if you got
me!
As said in the game of love,
Its better to have loved and lost
Then to have never played at all!

HAVE I EVER TOLD YOU WHY?

When the sun came up
And folded out of night!
I was still there, untouched, unbothered
Not a single muscle moved.
For it wasn't the pain, but the fear indeed,
It was the flashback, the shock
For how something so pure and kind
Turned into a ferocious act of a fickle mind.

I wondered Why? How and When?
I questioned my actions and deeds
For I wanted it to have a reason!
What went through your head
When that hand swung in the air.
When those curses poured out in despair.
But now I wonder the 'How' the most!
How will I ever get past the hurt!

How will I ever trust again,
How will I ever laugh and love again,
How will I ever be happy again
Perhaps I would never know!
But at least you know now
Where my guards up come from.

Here is my word when I say,
Have I ever told you why?

FASHION FAUX PAS OR IS IT?

I live in a world,
Where clothes define your worth.
Only New York understands
What New York wraps around the girth.

As I cross more avenues,
I get more intimidated.
Is it just me, Or,
Does everyone feel aligned?

Is it the clothes or the confidence
That I can't match up with.
I get immersed in the tribe
But I question, Can I pull up the vibe?

Black coats, Black boots, Black coffees
People with cases walking as if somewhere to
be.
Red gloves, Green pants, Purple hats
Groups wandering aimlessly at the Washington
curbs.

Best part of New York is that
No one gives a damn!
There is no right or wrong, only unique
As it should be, like a freaky cat!

Its the thought of wanting to be like that
Wanting to find my voice and my stye,
Its the fashion I strive to up my game
Wanting to present my true self without shame!

SUNSHINE SUNDAYS!

Pancake frostings, fluffed up eggs
Butter melting in the pan,
Its the smell of Sunday morning
For its half past ten.

Breakfast in bed,
Not a care for the clock ticking,
Its an easy day, not so lazy for sure
Warm showers waiting for their call.

Vacuum sweeps, trash unload
Sink emptied and catching up with the lads,
Grocery runs, laundry drops
It's these mundane events that now fill up my heart.

Sunday rituals, Waterfront walks
Cleanses my soul and so does my mind,
With every step, I see my growth
I see how far, I made it among the tide.

Its the sense of pride,
The joy of taking a breathe,
While the city keeps churning
Right before my glare.

SELF LOVE!

She is the fire, as her name,
She is the calm, as people shame.

She is the forest, with its own wild skill,
She is the ground, holding the depth within!

She looks beautiful and pristine
As absolutely serene,
As oceanside moonlight beam
Shining on the lost and unseen!

She reclaimed the throne,
She recalled and mourned,
How silly of her to forget
She is the love of her own!

She is the Queen, all love and trust,
Bow down! Cause She swallows and doesn't
leave the crust!

A LONE STONE!

Life lately has been on an overdrive.
It has its highest highs and lowest lows.
Only when I start believing life is getting good,
I am made aware of my situation as a whole.

Alone, detached, unnourished and deprived of
mothers love,
I am sick of pretending to be strong, not only for
me
But for everyone else dependent on me.
While in reality I am just one step away from a
non revivable collapse.

I can't even ask God to help me get my life
together,
cause It seems like it is but not how I want it to
be.
You ask who is stopping you from living the life
you want,
I swear, wish I had an answer for you.

Its not like I am not trying
but I am giving up way before I see the
potential.

I thought time heals, but time just makes you indifferent.
You never heal, you just try to forget and move on.

I have been waiting for my time to come.
I am loosing patience but trying to hang in there for as long as I can before I quit. I don't want to quit,
But I think I am close to being numb.

ME FOR ME, NOT FOR YOU!

"I was always the smart one,
First pick, not so shy, but the most
misunderstood;
May be because I have always been "Bold"
Carefree - True - Myself.

Unlike everyone else who thinks
Its so uncool - unnatural - unacceptable;
To not fit in a society that
Accepts conformity and declines originality!"

IT IS ABOUT TIME!

Its time to wash away my fears
and drench myself in hope and shine!

Its time to wake up from the dream
and make it happen in real time!

Its time to write the song
and to actually live the lyrics!

Its time to take actions
and not regret them later!

Its time to finally let go
and be in my own skin again!

Its time to live the city
and make the most in its prime!

TIME THAT FLEW!

Time flew by
Without a single apology,
Spring did not wait
And took the shivers with it!

Leaves bloomed back
Leaving early sunsets behind,
Sun smiled at me
As the beach opened it arm!

I was rejuvenated,
Eyes beaming with gold,
Lips thirsty as hell
Craving the freedom I so long lost!

It's the right moment
At the right place in the right time,
For I am in New York City
And it saved me from the fall!

www.ingramcontent.com/pod-product-compliance
Lightning Source LLC
La Vergne TN
LVHW010947200726
843509LV00013B/2310